Living with Quotes from the Dead

Tomi Saga

For my dear, brave and adventurous, mother and father.

INTRODUCTION

Throughout history, there have been philosophers and humorists with great minds. With pen and paper in hand, they composed splendid words of wit and wisdom that we may use to live, laugh, and think about.

Most of the quotes I've chosen for this book were spoken or written by people who have died. But their spirits and words live on—to guide us and cheer us through life's journey.

Contents

Some Word Meanings

What do these initials stand for?

BCE – Means before the Common Era (corresponds with years BC).

BC – Means before Christ or the years before Jesus Christ's estimated birth.

AD – Stands for "anno Domini" in Medieval Latin, meaning the years after the birth of Jesus.

Polymath – Is a person of wide-ranging knowledge or learning.

Philosophy – Comes from the Greek word "love of wisdom."
Philosopher – Is anyone who has a love of wisdom.

Stoic Philosopher – Stoicism is an ancient Greek and Roman philosophy that focused on wisdom, justice, courage, and moderation as a way of life.

Proverb – A short, clever saying that offers wisdom about life in some way.

On Health

Let food be thy medicine and medicine be thy food.

- Hippocrates
Greek physician and philosopher. Founding father of clinical
medicine and surgery
Born circa 460 BC

The only way to keep your health is to eat what you don't want, drink what you don't like, and do what you'd rather not.

- Mark Twain
American author and humorist
Born November 30, 1835

Happiness is good health and a bad memory.

\- Ingrid Bergman
Swedish actress
Born August 29, 1915

Health is the greatest of human blessings.

\- Hippocrates

On Life

The art of living is more like wrestling than dancing. For it requires that we should stand ready to meet on sets which are sudden and unexpected.

- Marcus Aurelius
Roman emperor and stoic philosopher
Born April 26, 121 AD

Live your life in such a way that you would not be ashamed to sell your parrot to the town gossip.

- Will Rogers
American actor, humorist and social commentator
Born November 4, 1879

Enjoy life. There's plenty of time to be dead.

> \- Hans Christian Andersen
> *Danish author*
> *Born April 2, 1805*

There is more to life than increasing its speed.

> \- Mohandas Gandhi
> *Indian lawyer, independence leader, and philosopher*
> *Born October 2, 1869*

Life is a school where time is the teacher and experience is the class.

> \- Yousef Elsagga
> *American father, husband, and businessman*
> *Born 1945*

Life consists not in holding good cards but playing those you hold well.

- Josh Billings
American humorist and lecturer
Born April 21, 1818

ON PEOPLE

Nothing so needs reforming as other people's habits.

- Mark Twain

Whenever people agree with me, I feel I must be wrong.

- Oscar Wilde
Irish author, poet, and playwright
Born October 16, 1854

There is no revenge so complete as forgiveness.

- Josh Billings

ON TRAVELING

Life is short, take the unplanned trip.

- Unknown

I have found that there ain't no surer way to find out whether you like people or hate them, than to travel with them.

- Mark Twain

ON ATTITUDE

Believe there is great power silently working all things for good, behave yourself, and never mind the rest.

- Beatrix Potter
English author and illustrator of Peter Rabbit books
Born July 28, 1866

Life is 10 percent what happens to me and 90 percent how I react to it.

- Lou Holtz
American college football coach
Born January 6, 1937

Character, not circumstance, makes the man.

\- Booker T. Washington
American educator and author
Born April 5, 1856

Things turn out best for the people who make the best of the way things turn out.

-John Wooden
Legendary basketball coach and player
Born October 14, 1910

Talent is God given. Be humble. Fame is man given. Be grateful. Conceit is self-given. Be careful.

-John Wooden

ON WORK / SUCCESS

To provide a good living for himself and family is the very first duty of every man.

- William Cobbett
English farmer, politician, and journalist
Born March 9, 1763

Hard work never killed anybody, but why take a chance?

- Edgar Bergen
American comedian
Born February 16, 1903

If opportunity doesn't knock, build a door.

\- Milton Berle
American actor and comedian
Born July 12, 1908

I've tried relaxing, but—I don't know—I feel more comfortable tense.

\- William Hamilton
American cartoonist and playwright
Born June 2, 1939

Try not to be a man of success, but rather a man of value.

\- Albert Einstein
Polymath, physicist, philosopher, and violin player
Born March 14, 1879

The reward of a thing well done is to have done it.

> \- Ralph Waldo Emerson
> *American author and philosopher*
> *Born May 25, 1803*

I see no virtues where I smell no sweat.

> \- Francis Quarles
> *English poet*
> *Born May 8, 1592*

A journey of a thousand miles begins with a single step.

> -Confucius
> *Chinese philosopher and political thinker*
> *Born September 28, 551 BC*

Nothing will work unless you do.

> -John Wooden

On School / Knowledge / Progress

Let others praise ancient times; I am glad I was born in these.

- Ovid
Roman poet
Born March 20, 43 BC

Computers are useless. They only give you answers.

- Pablo Picasso
Spanish painter
Born October 25, 1881

The important thing for you is not how much you know, but the quality of what you know.

- Desiderius Erasmus
Dutch theologian, Catholic priest, and scholar
Born October 27, 1469

What is algebra exactly? Is it those three cornered-things?

- James Barrie
Scottish novelist and playwright
Born May 9, 1860

The art of not reading is extremely important. It consists in not taking an interest in whatever may be engaging the attention of the general public at any particular time.

- Arthur Schopenhauer
German philosopher
Born February 22, 1788

On Men / Women / Love / Marriage

I do love nothing in the world so well as you.

- William Shakespeare
English playwright and poet
Born April 23, 1564

The proper basis for marriage is a mutual misunder-
standing.

- Oscar Wilde

The Fust thing a man duz in the morning iz to feel for
his pocket book, and the Fust thing a woman duz, is to
see if the looking glass iz all right.

- Josh Billings

When you go to your husband's house, do not behave well, for whatever you do will be wrong in any case.

- Advice from a Chinese Han Dynasty mother,
circa 206 BC

They say all marriages are made in heaven, but so are thunder and lightning.

\- Clint Eastwood
American actor and filmmaker
Born May 31, 1930

ON POSSESSIONS

An object in possession seldom retains the same charm as it had in pursuit.

- Gaius Plinius Segundos
Roman author, lawyer, commander, and magistrate
Born 61 AD

Ninety percent of everything is crap.

- Theodore Sturgeon
American author
Born February 26, 1918

The higher a monkey climbs, the more you see of its behind.

> \- Joseph Stilwell
> *US Army general*
> *Born March 19, 1883*

Simplicity is the ultimate sophistication.

> \- Leonardo da Vinci
> *Italian polymath, artist, inventor*
> *Born April 15, 1452*

Waste not, want not.

> \- Richard Edwards
> *English lyricist and playwright*
> *Born March 25, 1525*

The greatest wealth is to live content with little.

-Plato
Greek theorist and thinker
Born circa 427 BC

The best and most beautiful things in the world cannot
be seen or even touched, they must be felt with the heart.

- Helen Keller
American author, activist and disability rights advocate
Born June 27,1880

On Friends

Whenever you feel the need or wish to cheer yourself, think about all of the good qualities of those who are around you. The energy of one, for instance, the modesty of another, the generosity of a third, and some other gift of a fourth. For nothing is so ever cheering as the images of the qualities shining through in the character of those who live with us ... Have these images then, ever before your eyes.

- Marcus Aurelius

Friends come and go, but enemies accumulate.

- Arthur Bloch
American writer and author
Born January 1, 1948

Associate yourself with people of good quality, for it is better to be alone than in bad company.

- Booker T. Washington

Be who you are and say what you feel. Because those who mind don't matter and those who matter don't mind.

- Bernard Baruch
American statesman and financier
Born August 19, 1870

ON FAMILY / KIDS

Before I got married, I had six theories about bringing up children; now I have six children and no theories.

> \- John Wilmot
> *English poet and satirist*
> *Born April 1, 1647*

There are three ways to get things done: do it yourself, hire someone, or forbid your kids to do it.

> \- Monta Crane
> *American writer*
> *Born March 30, 1911*

When the first baby laughed for the first time, its laugh broke into a thousand pieces and they all went skipping about, and that was the beginning of fairies.

- James Barrie
Scottish novelist and playwright
Born May 9, 1860

If you want to make the world a better place, go home and love your family.

- Mother Teresa
Macedonia-born saint and Nobel Peace Prize winner
Born August 26, 1910

On War

Be wary of the man who urges action in which he himself incurs no risk.

- Joaquin de Setanti
Spanish military man, politician, writer, and philosopher
Born 1540

"

On Truth / Lies

੭ತಿ

When you want to help people, you tell them the truth. When you want to help yourself, you tell them what they want to hear.

- Thomas Sowell
American economist and economic historian
Born June 30, 1930

Honesty is a very expensive gift. Don't expect it from cheap people.

- Warren Buffett
American investor
Born August 30, 1930

There are only two ways of telling the complete truth—
anonymously and posthumously.

- Thomas Sowell

There is only one thing about which I am certain, and
that is that there is very little about one can be certain.

- W. Somerset Maugham
English author and playwright
Born January 25, 1874

ON STUPIDITY

Wise men speak because they have something to say;
fools, because they have to say something.

- Plato

Never miss a good chance to shut up.

- Will Rogers

God is good but never dance in a small boat.

- Irish proverb

One person can be pretty dumb sometimes, but for real bona fide stupidity, there ain't nothing can beat teamwork.

- Edward Abbey
American author
Born January 29, 1927

When in doubt, look intelligent.

- Garrison Keillor
American author and humorist
Born August 7, 1942

It is better to remain silent at the risk of being thought a fool than to talk and remove all doubt of it.

- Maurice Switzer
American author
Born October 16, 1870

If you find yourself in a hole, stop digging.

- Will Rogers

ON GOD / SADNESS / DEATH / GRIEVING / HEAVEN AND HELL

May God hold you gently in the palm of his hand. May you be in heaven a full half hour before the devil knows you're dead.

- Irish blessing

God helps those who dare.

-Ovid

The Hodja was considered the most learned man in his town. Everyone called on him for information and advice. One day a number of people called and demanded a reply to this question: "When, O Hodja, will be the end of the world?"

"Oh!" says he, "ask me something difficult. That is very easy to answer, when my wife dies, it will be the end of half of the world; when I die, then the whole world will end."

- Samuel Sullivan Cox
American congressman, diplomat, and author
Born September 30, 1824

When down in the mouth, remember Jonah. He came out all right.

- Thomas Edison
American inventor and businessman
Born February 11, 1847

There is no cure for birth and death save to enjoy the interval.

- George Santayana
Spanish novelist and philosopher
Born December 16, 1863

I don't want to go to heaven, none of my friends are there.

\- Oscar Wilde

We are all compounds of innumerable lives, each a sum in an infinite addition—the dead are not dead, they live in all of us, and move us, stirring faintly in every heartbeat.

\- Lafcadio Hearn
Greek born writer, translator and teacher
Born June 27, 1850

When you were born, you cried and the whole world rejoiced. Live your life in such a manner that when you die, the world cries and you rejoice.

\- Ancient Cherokee Indian proverb

On Pets

A dog is the only thing on earth that loves you more than he loves himself.

- Josh Billings

Dogs come when they're called; cats take a message and get back to you.

- Missy Camp Dizick
American author
Born October 3, 1959

ON CREATIVITY / ART

Imagination is more important than knowledge.
Knowledge is limited. Imagination encircles the world.

- Albert Einstein

I always ask the sitter if they want truth or flattery—
they always ask for truth, and I always give them flattery.

- Ruskin Spear
British portrait painter and art teacher
Born June 30, 1911

Modern art is what happens when painters stop
looking at girls and persuade themselves that they have a
better idea.

- John Ciardi
American poet and translator
Born June 24, 1916

There are three rules for writing a novel. Unfortunately,
no one knows what they are.

- W. Somerset Maugham

If you can't annoy somebody, there is little point in
writing.

- Kingsley Amis
English novelist
Born April 16, 1922

On the Earth

၅ာ

Civilization exists by geological consent, subject to change without notice.

\- Will James Durant
American historian, Pulitzer Prize winner, and philosopher
Born November 5, 1885

There is sufficiency in the world for man's need but not for man's greed.

\- Mohandas Gandhi

On Giving Thanks

Cultivate a habit of being grateful for every good thing that has come to you and give thanks continuously. And because all things have contributed to your advancement, you should include all things in your gratitude.

- Ralph Waldo Emerson